This book belongs to

_____

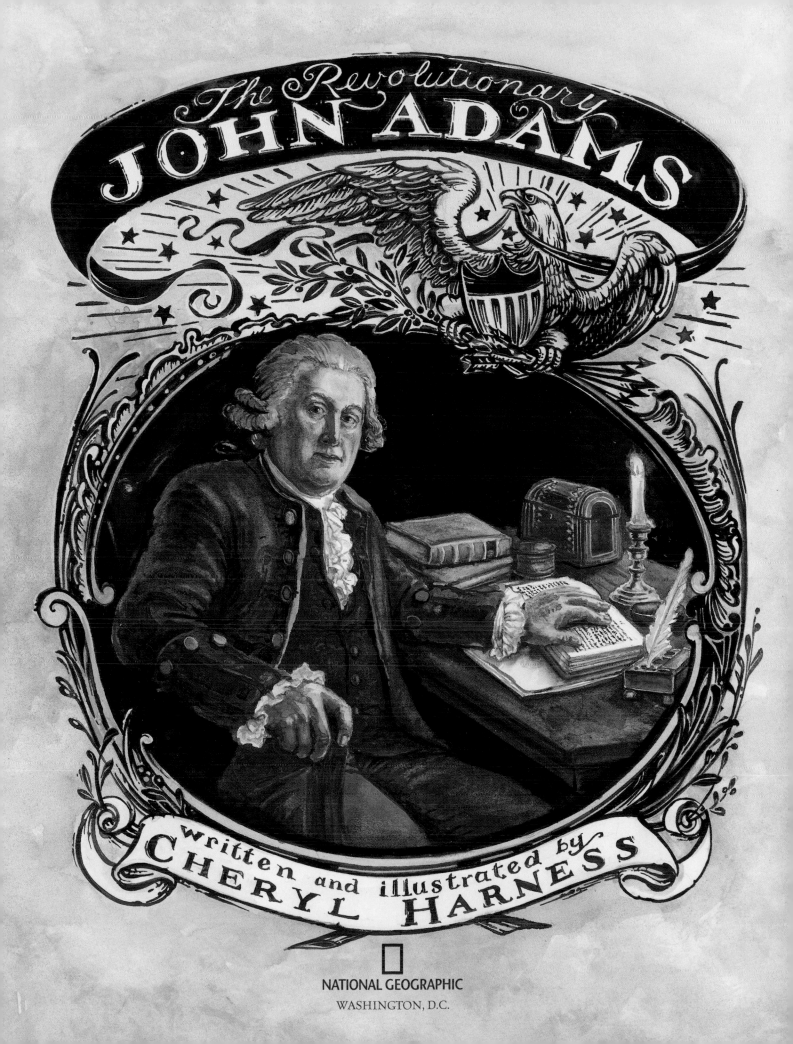

The Revolutionary
JOHN ADAMS

written and illustrated by
CHERYL HARNESS

NATIONAL GEOGRAPHIC

WASHINGTON, D.C.

There stands John Adams, the stout, stubborn New Englander eternally bookended and overshadowed by tall, glamorous Virginians. On one side, the reserved, heroic General George Washington, "first in the hearts of his countrymen." Imagine having to take up the Presidency—and keep a fragile republic in business—after that fellow! On the other is the cool, complicated genius of Monticello, Thomas Jefferson.

As Washington was the father of our country and Jefferson the author of its ideals, John Adams was the champion of its government. When the Congress was a brave group of men leading colonists through revolution to nationhood, John Adams was its leader. This very human Founding Father not only did more than anyone else when it came to imagining our checked-and-balanced government, he made nearly impossible wartime journeys to make sure that the American experiment would succeed. He kept the nation at peace and built up its navy so the Republic would survive. Not only did John and his heroic partner, Abigail, leave us a wealth of letters and a close-up look at their remarkable times, they began a dynasty of brilliant citizens: diplomats, historians, and even another President.

In the nation's capital, the sun glitters on stone monuments to George Washington and Thomas Jefferson. John Adams was every bit as brave as the former and as brilliant as the latter but there is—at this writing—no such monument for him. Perhaps this is fitting because stone is cold, and he was anything but. The United States is a proper, living monument to intense, cranky, warm, heart-on-his-sleeve John Adams—America's champion.

"I am well aware of the Toil and Blood and Treasure,
that it will cost Us to maintain this Declaration, and support and defend
these States—Yet through all the Gloom I can see Rays of ravishing
Light and Glory. I can see that the End is more than worth all the Means.
And that Posterity will triumph...."

JOHN ADAMS, PHILADELPHIA, PENNSYLVANIA, JULY 3, 1776

On the 19th of October 1735 in a cottage at the foot of Penn's Hill in the village of Braintree, not quite a mile from where the Atlantic Ocean meets the coast of New England, Susanna Adams had a son. He would be named John after his father, who was a shoemaker, a farmer, and a deacon in his church.

As the years went by, the family changed with two more sons, Peter and Elihu. The calendar changed, so John's birthday became October 30th. The village border changed, so his house became part of the town of Quincy in Massachusetts, which changed from a British colony to one of 13 states in a new nation. Why? Because the world changed, thanks in large part to John and Susanna's boy, John Adams, as he was known all the days of his remarkable life.

John's parents taught him to read when he was very small. They were proud of his bright progress until young John started skipping school. He made and sailed boats on the ponds and brooks where he swam and skated. He made kites and flew them high and deep into the sky above Penn's Hill. He stole away through the marsh grasses down below and waited, with his gun, for birds. He worked hard alongside his dad.

"Well, John," said Mr. Adams, "are you satisfied with being a farmer?"

John scraped the mud from his boots and said, "I like it very well, Sir."

"Ay, but I don't like it so well." Mr. Adams wanted him to go to college. They decided that John would do better at a private school down the road than with the cross, halfhearted village schoolmaster. In a little more than a year, 15-year-old John had a head full of Latin and mathematics and a stomach full of butterflies as he saddled his father's horse for the 4-hour, 12-mile ride to face the stiff-wigged, heavy-robed entrance examiners at Harvard College.

"Ran over the past Passages of my Life. Little Boats... whirly Giggs...Bows and Arrows, Guns, singing...."
J.A., MAY 31, 1760

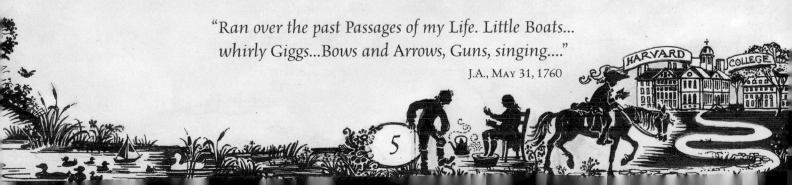

Earnest, friendly, curious John Adams fizzed with "total and complete happiness" at Harvard. He took himself very seriously. He'd scold himself for dreaming his life away, then dig into his books. After he and his 26 classmates graduated in 1755, John set off for Worcester, Massachusetts, and his first job as a teacher.

There, Schoolmaster Adams began studying with Lawyer Putnam and finding for himself "what is the proper Business of Mankind in this life?" On November 6, 1759, he was admitted to the bar in Boston. By then, Lawyer Adams of Braintree had met a frail, book-loving, brown-eyed parson's daughter in nearby Weymouth.

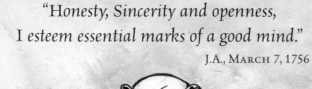

"Honesty, Sincerity and openness,
I esteem essential marks of a good mind."
J.A., MARCH 7, 1756

Over the next five years, many letters passed between John and this "dear girl," Abigail Smith. Sometimes he called her "Diana" after the goddess of the moon. In later years, he called her "Portia" after one of Shakespeare's heroines. John was her "dearest friend." Not long before her 20th birthday (on November 22) and John's 29th, they were married at her parents' house, October 25, 1764.

When his father died in 1761, John had inherited 40 acres of land, his mother's house, and the house next door, where he had his law office and made a home with his bride. What might the future hold for John and Abigail Adams?

"I lay in the well known Chamber, and dreamed I saw a Lady, tripping it over the Hills,...Spreading Light and Beauty and Glory all around her."

J.A. TO A. SMITH, AUGUST 1763

John Adams and Abigail Smith were married in her home in Weymouth, Massachusetts.

His Majesty KING GEORGE III

When the French and Indian War came to an end in 1763, young King George III and his Parliament in London decided to keep an army posted in the Colonies to protect British Americans from being attacked by Indians— and to keep the colonists out of the Native Americans' hunting grounds beyond the Appalachian Mountains. People began to grumble.

The colonists grumbled more in 1764, when Parliament came up with a 3¢ tax on every gallon of molasses to help pay for the army. In 1765, John and his wife cared for their first baby, Abigail ("Nabby"), and talked about the latest fateful news: All official papers and even playing cards must be stamped. More taxes! The colonists, who already had to provide beds, candles, and cider for the soldiers, were upset. Why? John spelled it out in an essay that would be read on both sides of the Atlantic Ocean. English citizens, whose forefathers had cleared this "inhospitable wilderness

Bostonians met under a century-old elm tree to protest the STAMP ACT. They hanged effigies of the King's ministers and tax collectors in its branches. Soon, almost every American town and village had its own "LIBERTY TREE."

Colonists wearing red, pointy "liberty caps" dangled real live tax collectors from the tops of "liberty poles" and, sometimes, the patriotic protesters covered their victims with hot tar and goose feathers.

TAX

"That enormous Engine, fabricated by the british Parliament,
for battering down all the Rights and Liberties of America,
I mean the Stamp Act, has raised and spread thro the whole Continent,
a Spirit that will be recorded to our Honour, with all future Generations."

J.A., BRAINTREE, DECEMBER 18, 1765

for the hope of liberty" had no say in Parliament about taxes they had to pay. Taxation without representation was a violation of common law.

The Stamp Act was done away with by the time Nabby's little brother John Quincy was born in 1767, but ships were on the way from England with word of new taxes for the Crown. Stubborn colonists stopped buying taxed paper, paint, glass, and tea. Patriotic hotheads tarred and feathered royal tax collectors. John's shabby, fiery cousin Sam Adams and his Sons of Liberty organized protests, as the King sent more red-coated soldiers—the hated "Lobsterbacks"—to police Boston. John moved his law office and his family into this bubbling pot of political excitement. Soon, another daughter, Susanna, began her tiny life in December 1768. Not long after she died in the deep winter of 1770, tensions boiled over on a cold, moonlit night in Boston.

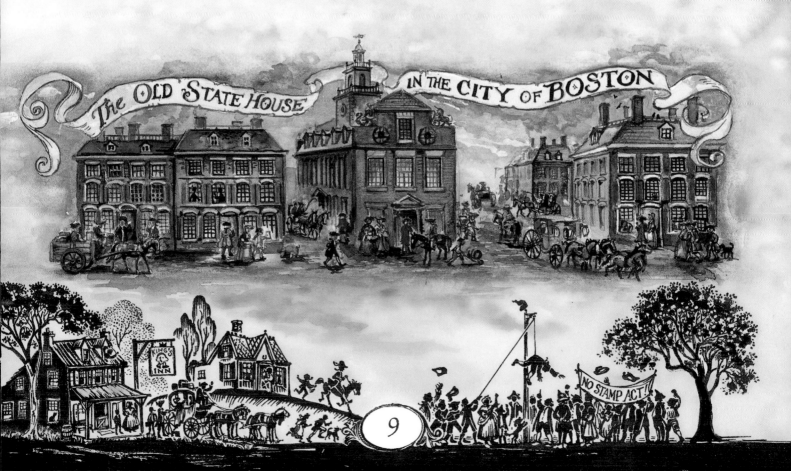

The Old State House in the City of Boston

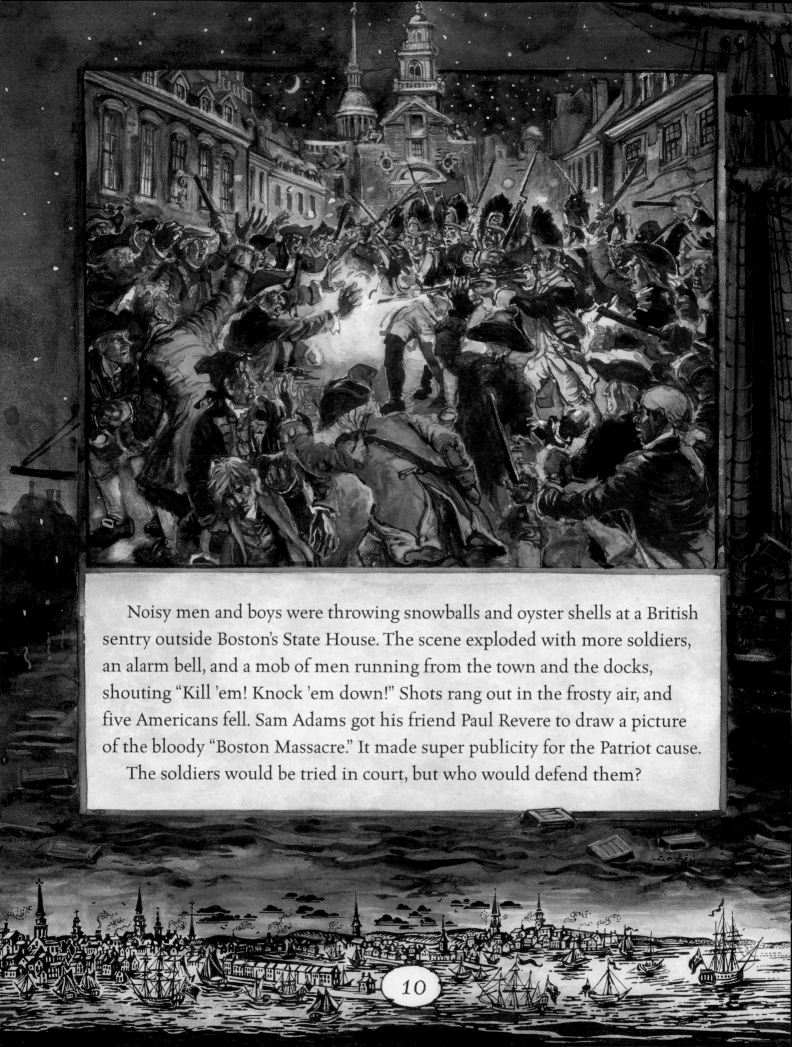

Noisy men and boys were throwing snowballs and oyster shells at a British sentry outside Boston's State House. The scene exploded with more soldiers, an alarm bell, and a mob of men running from the town and the docks, shouting "Kill 'em! Knock 'em down!" Shots rang out in the frosty air, and five Americans fell. Sam Adams got his friend Paul Revere to draw a picture of the bloody "Boston Massacre." It made super publicity for the Patriot cause. The soldiers would be tried in court, but who would defend them?

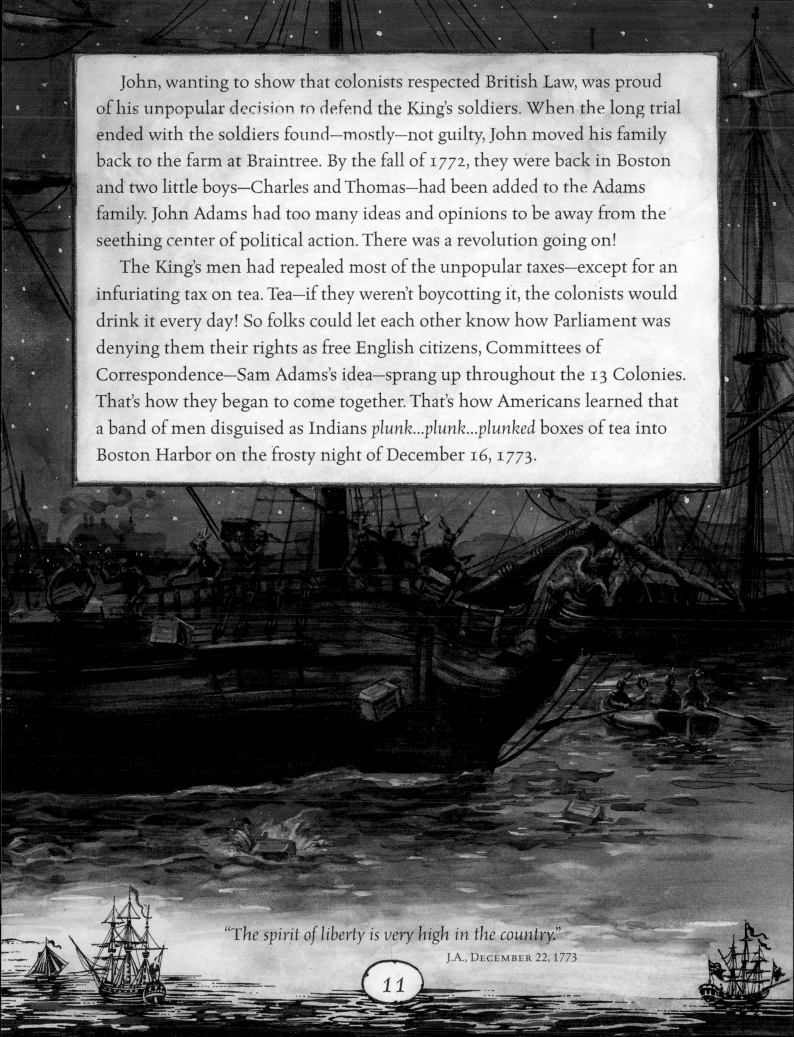

John, wanting to show that colonists respected British Law, was proud of his unpopular decision to defend the King's soldiers. When the long trial ended with the soldiers found—mostly—not guilty, John moved his family back to the farm at Braintree. By the fall of 1772, they were back in Boston and two little boys—Charles and Thomas—had been added to the Adams family. John Adams had too many ideas and opinions to be away from the seething center of political action. There was a revolution going on!

The King's men had repealed most of the unpopular taxes—except for an infuriating tax on tea. Tea—if they weren't boycotting it, the colonists would drink it every day! So folks could let each other know how Parliament was denying them their rights as free English citizens, Committees of Correspondence—Sam Adams's idea—sprang up throughout the 13 Colonies. That's how they began to come together. That's how Americans learned that a band of men disguised as Indians *plunk...plunk...plunked* boxes of tea into Boston Harbor on the frosty night of December 16, 1773.

"The spirit of liberty is very high in the country."

J.A., DECEMBER 22, 1773

11

"We live my dear Soul, in an Age of Tryal. What will be the Consequence I know not."

J.A. TO A.A., MAY 12, 1774

His Majesty George III, King of England, the world's greatest power, was very angry. He sent part of his huge navy to slam the port of Boston shut. No commerce in or out. Up and down the Colonies, printers, town criers, and couriers spread the news. This could happen to any harbor town, that was clear. Colonial delegates would meet on September 5, 1774, in a Continental Congress at Philadelphia, Pennsylvania, and figure out what to do next. "God grant us Wisdom," John wrote, "and Fortitude!"

On a summer day at Penn's Hill farm, John said good-bye to his family and neighbors. Soon he, Sam Adams, John Hancock, and the other Massachusetts delegates set off in a big, bumpy carriage to Philadelphia.

Philadelphia was the biggest, richest city in colonial America. John met hothead Patrick Henry, slender Richard Henry Lee, and tall George Washington of Virginia, witty Caesar Rodney of Delaware, and "pale as ashes" John Dickinson of Pennsylvania. The 56 men from 12 colonies got to know each other, argued, and feasted. The 13th colony, Georgia, sent no delegates but agreed to go along with the other delegates' decision: The colonists would stop trading with England.

"The Business of the Congress is tedious, beyond Expression. This Assembly is like no other that ever existed....every Man upon every Question must shew his oratory, his Criticism, and his Political Abilities. The Consequence of this is, that Business is drawn and spun out to an immeasurable Length."

J.A. TO A.A., OCTOBER 9, 1774

CARPENTERS' HALL

13

John Adams and the others had a lot to think about on their separate ways home over rutted trails, under canopies of bright October trees. John began publishing thoughtful essays about English liberties and the nature of government. When he heard what happened on the 19th of April, 1775, John put down his quill, saddled his horse, and galloped off to the villages of Lexington and Concord to see for himself where shots had been fired and men had died.

He knew that he must join the other delegates in Philadelphia and leave Abigail to care for their children and their farm. "In Case of real Danger," he wrote, "fly to the Woods with our Children. Give my tenderest Love to them."

The men of the Second Continental Congress had a gigantic to-do list. John Adams's voice was heard in committees assigned to these tasks: Make a navy. Fortify 1,500 miles of coastline. Raise a Continental Army. Feed, uniform, train, arm it, and pay it—somehow. Issue Continental currency. (Colonial money was scarce and differed plenty.) Find a commander for the army. John nominated "generous and brave" George Washington. "The Liberties of America," John wrote, "depend upon him."

"Our Hopes and Fears are alternately very strong."

J.A. TO A.A., JUNE 23, 1775

As he was writing these words to Abigail on June 17, 1775, she and seven-year-old John Quincy were standing on a hilltop back home in Braintree. They could hear the guns and see the smoke from the battle on the hills across the river from Boston. They cried for their friends who were dying there. Far away in Philadelphia, her husband wrote, "We have nothing to hope for from our loving Mother Country."

"It gives me more Pleasure than I can express to learn that you sustain with so much Fortitude, the Shocks and Terrors of the Times. You are really very brave, my dear, you are an Heroine."

J.A. TO A.A., JULY 7, 1775

King George's ships bottled up all of America's harbors as Patriots in homespun
clothes made do, drank anything but tea, drilled with muskets and their grandpas'
blunderbusses, and argued with their Tory neighbors, who were still loyal to the
Crown. American soldiers froze and failed to capture Quebec far away in Canada.
Folks buzzed over Thomas Paine's patriotic pamphlet, "Common Sense:" "for God's
sake, let us come to a final separation....The birthday of a new world is at hand."
The 13 very different Colonies were coming to see themselves as one America.
"The last Step" was coming to the top of the Congressmen's to-do list.

After much look-before-leaping debate, Mr. Lee of Virginia resolved that
"these United Colonies are, and of right ought to be, free and independent States."

"In the new Code of Laws which I suppose it will be necessary for you to make
I desire you would Remember the Ladies...."

A.A. to J.A., March 31, 1776

NABBY · JOHN QUINCY · CHARLES · TOMMY

Now there must be a proper manifesto. The delegates chose John Adams and New Yorker Robert R. Livingston, Roger Sherman of Connecticut, the world-famous inventor-publisher-scientist-Philadelphian Dr. Benjamin Franklin, and tall, red-headed Thomas Jefferson, a Virginian known to have a "masterly Pen." For two hot weeks in June 1776, his job was an inky struggle to find the exact noble words to say why colonists were defying their King and smashing the established order. Although much debated and edited, the lofty words of the Declaration of Independence sprang from this shy aristocrat. He was taller and nearly eight years younger than John Adams, the passionate leader of the Congress, but their names would always be linked in the legendary story of their nation's beginning.

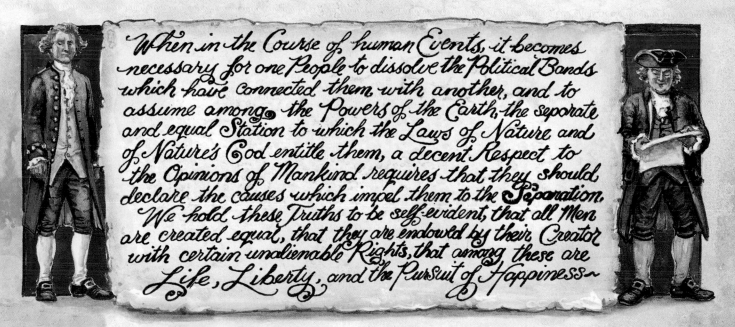

When in the Course of human Events, it becomes necessary for one People to dissolve the Political Bands which have connected them with another, and to assume among the Powers of the Earth, the separate and equal Station to which the Laws of Nature and of Nature's God entitle them, a decent Respect to the Opinions of Mankind requires that they should declare the causes which impel them to the Separation. We hold these Truths to be self-evident, that all Men are created equal, that they are endowed by their Creator with certain unalienable Rights, that among these are Life, Liberty, and the Pursuit of Happiness~

"When,...had three millions of people full power and a fair opportunity to form and establish the wisest and happiest government that human wisdom can contrive?"

J.A., MARCH 1776

17

On July 1, 1776, the delegates leaned forward, brushed flies from their silk stockings, and fanned their flushed faces as they listened to rain on the windows and John Adams's passionate, logical argument. His powerful speech lifted the delegates from their seats. Lee's resolution passed the next day, July 2nd, "to be solemnized with Pomp and Parade, with Shews, Games, Sports, Guns, Bells, Bonfires and Illuminations from one end of this Continent," far-sighted John wrote, "to the other from this Time forward forever more."

"God Save our American States and 3 cheers which rended the air, the Bells rang,
the privateers fired,...and every face appeard joyfull....the king's [coat of] arms
were taken down from the State House...and burnt in King Street.
Thus ends royall authority in this State, and all the people shall say Amen."

A.A. TO J.A., JULY 21, 1776

INDEPENDENCE!

As the delegates were voting for the Declaration on the 4th of July, a huge fleet of British warships was sighted off the coast of New York. The troops on board had orders to crush the American rebellion. Their bayonets glittered in the sun.

Abigail and the children were in Boston. They were all sick after being inoculated, a relatively new weapon against an old killer more deadly than guns: smallpox. When they heard the cheering, cannonfire, and church bells on the 18th of July, they knew that the Declaration of Independence had been read to the people of Boston from the balcony of the Old State House. Of course they knew all about it from "Pappa's" joyous letter.

Everyone knew that it was one thing to declare independence and entirely another to win it from an angry King. To see if the rash Americans would reconsider, His Lordship, Admiral Howe set up a meeting on Staten Island, near the city of New York. The Congress sent John, Ben Franklin, and Mr. Rutledge of South Carolina on the two-day journey.

On the first night, Mr. Adams had to share a bed with Dr. Franklin, who insisted that the window be open. John closed it—he'd catch cold with "the Air of the night blowing in upon me." "We shall be suffocated," said Franklin. So John opened the window, jumped into bed, and fell asleep as Franklin shared his "Theory of Colds."

The Admiral suggested that the Colonies honor and obey the King. No. The Patriots suggested a peace treaty between Britain and the Independent States of America. No. John's first assignment in diplomacy came to an end. England and America would have to fight it out. Shortly after the men returned to Philadelphia, they got word that the British had captured New York City on September 15. The Continental Army was in retreat. Americans needed help, and their best bet was England's old enemy, France. Seventy-year-old Ben Franklin set sail to Paris on a desperate mission.

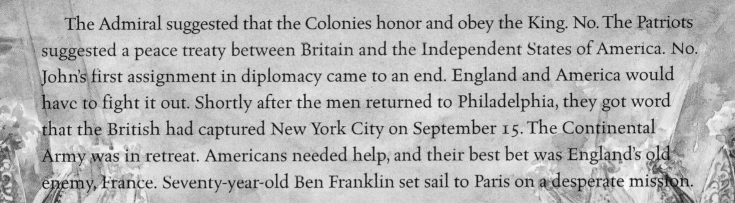

On the home front, John's monstrous job as head of Congress's War and Ordinance Committee was finding food, boots, medicine, money, gunpowder—all that General Washington needed for his all but impossible job: not losing the war. When John and the other delegates weren't running for their lives (the British captured Philadelphia in September 1777), they were drafting foreign treaties and designing a plan of government: the Articles of Confederation. Finally, worn-out, stressed-out John went home to see his family and do some lawyering.

"*The Events of War are uncertain. We cannot insure Success, but We can deserve it.*"

J.A. TO A.A., FEBRUARY 18, 1776

21

Not long after the Americans' huge victory over the British at Saratoga, New York, in October 1777, Congress asked John to set sail on a diplomatic mission of his own. For John and Abigail there was no choice. It was his patriotic duty to go, hers to stay behind. Young John Quincy would go with his father to observe and learn.

"Posterity! You will never know how much it cost the present Generation to preserve your Freedom! I hope you will make good Use of it. If you do not, I shall repent in Heaven that I ever took half the Pains to preserve it."

J.A. TO A.A., APRIL 26, 1777

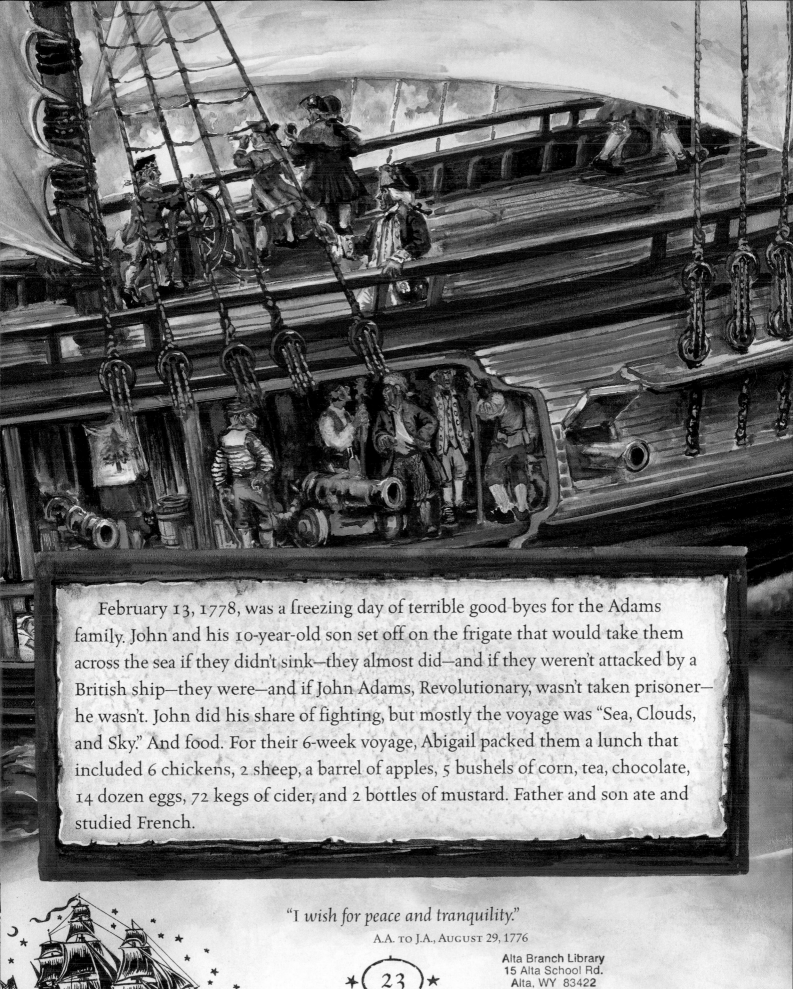

February 13, 1778, was a freezing day of terrible good-byes for the Adams family. John and his 10-year-old son set off on the frigate that would take them across the sea if they didn't sink—they almost did—and if they weren't attacked by a British ship—they were—and if John Adams, Revolutionary, wasn't taken prisoner—he wasn't. John did his share of fighting, but mostly the voyage was "Sea, Clouds, and Sky." And food. For their 6-week voyage, Abigail packed them a lunch that included 6 chickens, 2 sheep, a barrel of apples, 5 bushels of corn, tea, chocolate, 14 dozen eggs, 72 kegs of cider, and 2 bottles of mustard. Father and son ate and studied French.

"I wish for peace and tranquility."
A.A. TO J.A., AUGUST 29, 1776

They got an education in France, one in school, the other in the Paris of pudgy young Louis XVI and diamond-decked Marie Antoinette, where poverty surrounded "Delights." John Adams was surrounded with suave ministers, spies, theater, beauty, hidden meanings, politeness, and wily, slow-going, 72-year-old Benjamin Franklin, who was fabulously popular, especially with ladies. John plowed through diplomatic paperwork Franklin left undone and drafted

"This is a delicious Country."   J.A. TO A.A., JULY 26, 1778

reports to Congress, and in 1779 father and son sailed home across a summer sea.

Less than three months later, having taken the time to write the Massachusetts Constitution, John and Abigail parted again, for the sake of their country. John Quincy, his little brother Charles, and their father, the "Minister Plenipotentiary to negotiate Treaties of Peace (the Congress was being optimistic) and Commerce with Great Britain," sailed away.

"Dearest Friend...We shall yet be happy, I hope and pray...Yours, ever, ever yours,"

J.A. TO A.A., NOVEMBER 13, 1779

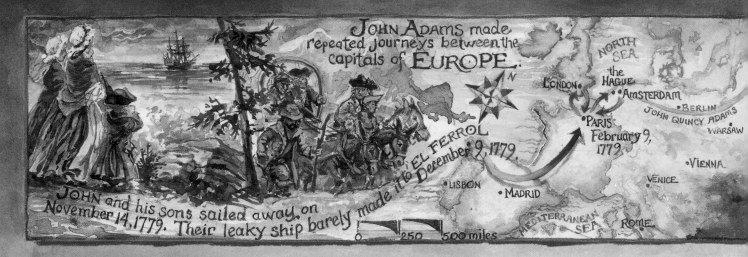

After nearly sinking in the Atlantic and surviving a mule caravan across Spain into France, John dug deep into his bag of political skills and patience and coaxed out of Holland official recognition and loans, lifeblood for his nation. While British forces were surrendering in Virginia on October 19, 1781, John Quincy, 14-year-old interpreter for the U.S. minister to Russia, was on an adventure of his own to the court of Empress Catherine the Great.

John, old Dr. Franklin, and John Jay negotiated the difficult peace and trade treaties with England and France. When the last papers were signed on September 3, 1783, twenty years of struggle and war came to an end. A new nation began.

John's "horrid Solitude" ended when John Quincy returned from Russia and Nabby and Abigail came to be with them in London. (Charles was back in

"I must go to you or you must come to me. I cannot live in this horrid Solitude...a Child was never more weary of a Whistle, than I am of Embassies."

J.A. TO A.A., MAY 14, 1782

Massachusetts with Thomas.) The happy family set off to Paris in the summer of 1784. They found old friends there: Thomas Jefferson and his daughter Patsy.

For all of the difficulties and wonders that they experienced in Europe, the moment most roundly packed with mixed feelings came on June 1, 1785, when John Adams of Boston, first U.S. ambassador to England, was introduced to the King. Trembling with emotion, George III met the "friendship of the United States as an independent power."

Four years later, the feelings must have been pure joy. After nearly nine years away, a bald, portly, 53-year-old Patriot returned to peaceful, independent America. On June 17, 1788, a huge crowd gave a hero's welcome to 43-year-old Abigail Adams and her "dearest friend," home at last.

"Indeed I have seen enough of the world, small as [it] has been, and shall be content to learn what is further to be known from the page of History."

A.A., MAY 1, 1788

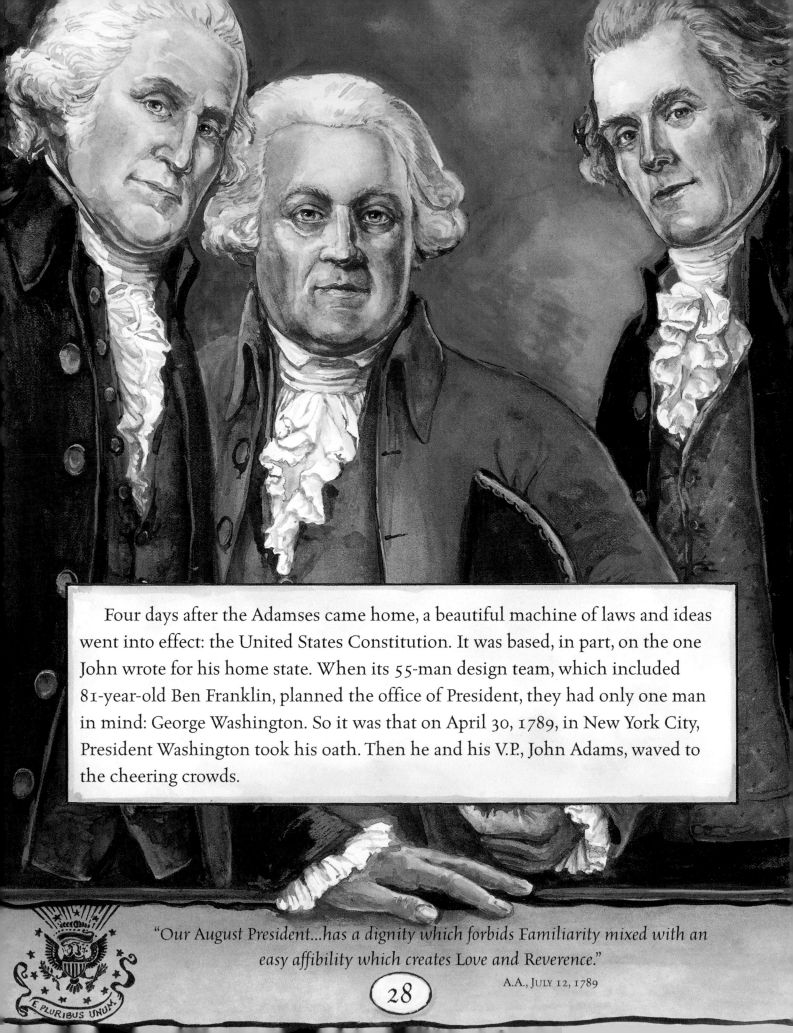

Four days after the Adamses came home, a beautiful machine of laws and ideas went into effect: the United States Constitution. It was based, in part, on the one John wrote for his home state. When its 55-man design team, which included 81-year-old Ben Franklin, planned the office of President, they had only one man in mind: George Washington. So it was that on April 30, 1789, in New York City, President Washington took his oath. Then he and his V.P., John Adams, waved to the cheering crowds.

"Our August President...has a dignity which forbids Familiarity mixed with an easy affibility which creates Love and Reverence."

A.A., JULY 12, 1789

E PLURIBUS UNUM

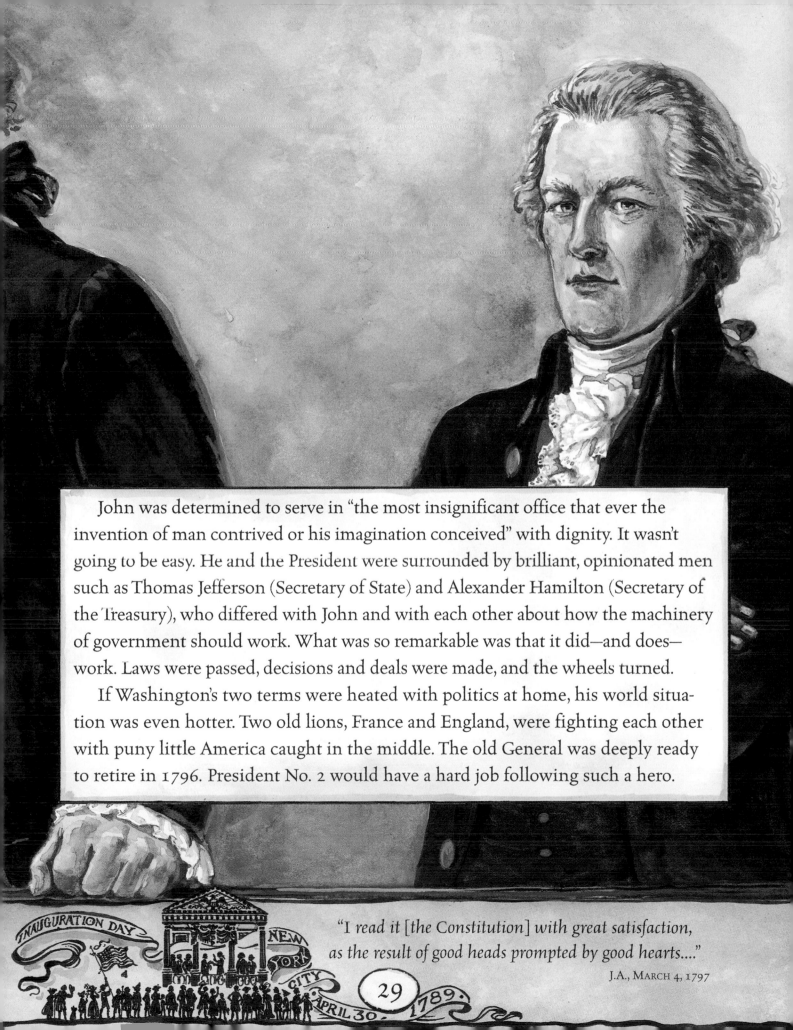

John was determined to serve in "the most insignificant office that ever the invention of man contrived or his imagination conceived" with dignity. It wasn't going to be easy. He and the President were surrounded by brilliant, opinionated men such as Thomas Jefferson (Secretary of State) and Alexander Hamilton (Secretary of the Treasury), who differed with John and with each other about how the machinery of government should work. What was so remarkable was that it did—and does—work. Laws were passed, decisions and deals were made, and the wheels turned.

If Washington's two terms were heated with politics at home, his world situation was even hotter. Two old lions, France and England, were fighting each other with puny little America caught in the middle. The old General was deeply ready to retire in 1796. President No. 2 would have a hard job following such a hero.

"I read it [the Constitution] with great satisfaction, as the result of good heads prompted by good hearts...."

J.A., MARCH 4, 1797

INAUGURATION DAY · NEW YORK CITY · APRIL 30. 1789.

29

General ✚ OLIVER ELLSWORTH, Chief Justice of the SUPREME COURT ✚ JOHN ADAMS, President ✚ THOS. JEFFERSON, Vice President ✚ TIMOTHY PICKERING, Secretary of State ✚ OLIVER WOLCOTT, Jr., Secretary of the Treasury ✚ JAMES McHENRY, Secretary of War ✚ CHARLES LEE, Attorney

In 1796, the race between Federalist John Adams and Democratic-Republican Thomas Jefferson was the first big game in American hardball party politics. John won it—barely. According to the Constitution, Jefferson as runner-up would be Vice President. On the 4th of March, 1797, George Washington stepped aside for John Adams, the second in a still-unbroken line of leaders elected by the citizens of their government. Except for political bickering—the nation's permanent background grumble—this passing of power was peaceful and a huge, historic step for mankind.

John inherited the first President's French and English problems. King Louis XVI had sent help for America's struggle, but nothing could save him or his corrupt

"A solemn scene it was indeed, and it was made more affecting to me by the presence of the General, whose countenance was as serene and unclouded as the day. Methought I heard him say, "Ay! I am fairly out and you fairly in! See which of us will be happiest.""

J.A. TO A.A., MARCH 5, 1797

government when revolution smashed through his country. Now France's fierce young leader, Napoleon Bonaparte, demanded U.S. help in his war against England. Vice President Jefferson and plenty of other Americans passionately agreed even though France was capturing American ships and demanding bribe money in exchange for peace. Other folks noisily demanded war with France and leaned toward their enemy's enemy, England—even though that country was also seizing American ships at sea. Federalists in the Congress passed laws to put pro-French, anti-government protesters in jail or, if they were foreigners, out of the country.

John Adams knew that to keep his nation afloat, he had to keep it neutral, which seemed to please nobody. "Mr. Adams is vain, irritable, stubborn," Vice President Jefferson was heard to say. To keep America safe, John ordered new warships, created a Department of the Navy, and sent peace negotiators to Paris. Then, just before Christmas 1799, came news that plunked like a round black stone into the world of John and Abigail Adams. George Washington was dead. The tumultuous 18th century and a chapter in the story of America was coming to an end.

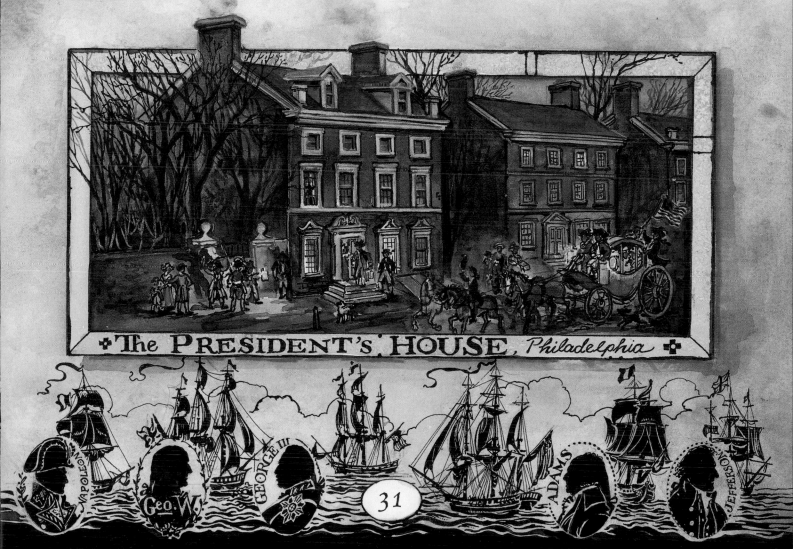

The PRESIDENT'S HOUSE, *Philadelphia*

The Adamses had known for a long time that they and the U.S. government were going to be moving from Philadelphia to the "Federal City" of Washington. On Saturday afternoon, November 1, 1800, four horses pulled a coach along mud-rutted, stump-stubbled Pennsylvania Avenue and up to an unfinished sandstone mansion, the biggest house in America. Sixty-five-year-old John Adams stepped out and gazed up at his new home, which would be forever known as the White House. His wife and granddaughter, 4-year-old Susanna, arrived two weeks later, having gotten lost in the "Forest & woods on the way."

In their new home, they kept close to the fireplaces. The lofty, hardly furnished rooms smelled of smoke, damp plaster, sawdust, and paint. Abigail, who didn't want citizens gawking at the First Family's linen drying in the yard, would have laughed to know that her East Room clothesline would become a White House legend.

"I pray Heaven to bestow the best of Blessings
on this House and All that shall hereafter inhabit.
May none but honest and wise Men ever rule under this Roof."

J.A. TO A.A., NOVEMBER 2, 1800

In December, the Adamses got word that their son Charles had died and that John had lost the very nasty election of 1800. On January 1, 1801, a calm George Washington looked out from his golden frame at curious citizens who'd come to eat sweets, sip tea, and greet the President and Mrs. Adams. Their New Year's Day reception began a holiday tradition that would last more than a hundred years.

Before the sun came up on President Jefferson's Inauguration Day, March 4, 1801, the second President climbed aboard a northbound stagecoach. There is no record that John was invited to watch his sometime friend and political rival take his oath of office. Besides, John Adams was anxious to get home to Braintree, to stay.

The Adamses spent the rest of their long lives in a house they named Peacefield. Old farmer John called it Stonyfield. He tramped over the countryside where a sturdy hooky-playing boy once sailed boats and flew kites. John built stone fences, tended his cornfields and fruit trees, and read stacks of books. He and Abigail took pride in their oldest son's career, as John Quincy became Senator, Minister to Russia, and President Monroe's stern Secretary of State. They looked after grandchildren and worried over Thomas, who grew up to be an unhappy man, and, most of all, their much-loved Nabby, who came home to suffer and die of cancer in 1813.

"Death is sweeping his scythe all around us,
cutting down our old friends and brandishing it over us."

J.A. TO J.Q.A., JUNE 10, 1816

Four generations of Adamses

Five years later and three days after their 54th wedding anniversary, two old partners separated one last time, except now it was John who was left behind when the "dear partner" of his life died on the 28th of October, 1818.

"The bitterness of death is past. The grim spider so terrible to human nature has no sting for me. My consolations are more than I can number.... The pangs and anguish have not been so great as when you and I embarked for France in 1778."

J.A. TO J.Q.A., NOVEMBER 10, 1818

35

Sitting at his writing desk or in his big red chair, John found much comfort in his written conversations that the postmen carried between John and his family and friends such as the Marquis de Lafayette who, as a young French nobleman, fought for America's liberty, and Dr. Benjamin Rush, a signer of the Declaration of Independence. In many a letter, the doctor encouraged his two stubborn friends, Adams and Jefferson, to set aside their hard feelings and write to each other. Finally, on New Year's Day, 1812, John picked up a quill with his trembling hand and wrote a letter to his old comrade 500 miles away in Virginia—as the eagle flies.

The two Revolutionaries, who had seen and made so much history, exchanged 158 letters over the next 14 years. "You and I," John wrote, "ought not to die before We have explained ourselves to each other." The letters were full of their memories and thoughts about books, revolutions, education, slavery, war, politics and philosophy, their sadnesses—and their triumphs: Jefferson's design of the University of Virginia; John Quincy Adams's becoming the sixth President of the United States.

"A letter from you calls up recollections very dear to my mind. It carried me back to the times when, beset with difficulties and dangers, we were fellow laborers in the same cause, struggling for what is most valuable to man, his rights of self-government."

T.J. TO J.A., JANUARY 21, 1812

They wrote about their failing health as well. John was too frail to go to his son's inauguration in 1825. Both old men were determined to live on until the summer of 1826, so they did. Men from town came and asked John for a few words to say on the big celebration coming up. He told them, "Independence forever!"

The two old Patriots passed away on the day of the Great and Miraculous

Coincidence, on the Glorious Fourth of July, 1826. On the evening of the 50th anniversary of the first Independence Day, as citizens around the nation were firing up speeches, bonfires, and cannon, John whispered, "Thomas Jefferson survives." But no, the 83-year-old "Pen of the Revolution" had already gone a few hours before the passing of his old friend, 90-year-old John Adams, the Revolution's tireless "Voice."

"I look back with rapture to those golden days when Virginia and Massachusetts lived and acted together like a band of brothers."

J.A. TO T.J., FEBRUARY 25, 1825

THE WORLD
OF
PRESIDENT
John Adams
1797 & 1801

IN DISPUTE
Part of
MASS.

L. SUPERIOR

BRITISH TERRITORY
CANADA

N.H.
VT.
MASS.
R.I.
CONN.
N.J.

OREGON

L. MICHIGAN
L. HURON
L. ONTARIO
L. ERIE

N.Y.
PENN.
DEL.
WASHINGTON
D.C.

MEXICO

(SPANISH
TERRITORY)

MISSISSIPPI RIVER

MISSOURI RIVER

OHIO RIVER

INDIANA
Territory

NORTH-
WEST
Territory

MD.

VA.

KY.

N.C.

LOUISIANA
(FRENCH
TERRITORY)

TENN.

TERRITORY
CLAIMED BY
GEORGIA

GA.

S.C.

MISSISSIPPI
TERRITORY

MEXICO

SPANISH
TERRITORY: FLORIDA

ATLANTIC OCEAN

GULF OF MEXICO

BAHAMA
ISLANDS

PACIFIC OCEAN

TROPIC OF CANCER

THE
UNITED STATES
and TERRITORIES
IN 1800
scale of miles
0 100 200 300 400 500
STATE and TERRITORIAL
CAPITALS ★

38

1797

★ Vienna, Austria: Composer Franz Schubert is born.

★ New Haven, Conn.: Eli Whitney, inventor of the cotton gin, begins manufacturing muskets with his new "American System" and becomes the father of mass production.

★ London, England: John Quincy Adams marries Louisa Catherine Johnson, July 26.

★ Boston, Mass.: The warship USS *Constitution*, also called "Old Ironsides," is launched, Oct. 21. She will survive many battles. Today she is the oldest battleship afloat in any of the world's navies.

★ Hundreds of U.S. ships are being captured at sea by French vessels. When President Adams sends men to Paris to work something out, they are met by three government agents, known as X, Y, & Z. They demand money in exchange for French respect of the U.S. flag. The XYZ Affair makes many Americans furious at France.

★ Paris, France: Andre Garnerin makes the world's first parachute jump—from a hot-air balloon, Oct. 22.

1798

★ Napoleon Bonaparte and his French Army invade Egypt. They win the Battle of the Pyramids, seize the island of Malta, then take over the Kingdom of Naples in Italy.

★ Charenton, France: Painter Eugene Delacroix is born, April 26.

★ Germany: Aloys Senefelder invents a way of printing known as lithography.

★ U.S. Congress passes the notorious Alien and Sedition Acts meant to quiet political opposition. The Department of the Navy is established as well as the Mississippi Territory.

1799

★ Ireland: A failed rebellion eventually leads Ireland to become part of Great Britain in 1801.

★ Egypt: A French officer discovers a big black stone. The letters carved on this "Rosetta Stone" will be the key to deciphering the hieroglyphic language of ancient Egypt.

★ France: Napoleon becomes First Consul, Nov. 9

★ Siberia: A mummified mammoth is discovered.

★ Mt. Vernon, Va.: George Washington dies, Dec. 14.

1800

★ The U.S. Library of Congress is established.

★ Vienna, Austria: Ludwig von Beethoven completes his First Symphony.

★ Spain cedes the Louisiana Territory to France.

★ President Adams appoints William H. Harrison (9th President) governor of the Indiana Territory.

★ John Adams becomes the first occupant of the White House, Nov. 1.

★ Long Island, New York: President Adams's son Charles dies, Nov. 30.

1801

★ A slave revolt is crushed in Virginia. The leader, Gabriel, is hanged, Oct. 30.

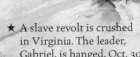

★ The 19th Century begins.

★ U.S. population: five million

To Vicki Grove and the BiblioBabes —CH

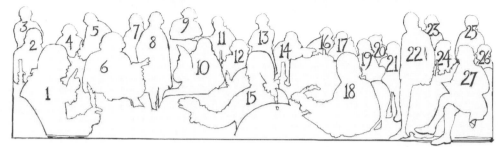

Key to the painting of the Second Continental Congress, pages 14–15: 1. John Adams, Mass.; 2. Samuel Adams, Mass.; 3. Roger Sherman, Conn.; 4. George Read, Del.; 5. Josiah Bartlett, N.H.; 6. Elbridge Gerry, Mass.; 7. William Livingston, N.J.; 8. William Paca, Md.; 9. John Hancock, Mass.; 10. Benjamin Franklin, Penn.; 11. John Jay, N.Y.; 12. James Wilson, Penn.; 13. Thomas McKean, Del.; 14. Stephen Hopkins, R.I.; 15. John Dickinson, Penn.; 16. John Langdon, N.H.; 17. Caesar Rodney, Del.; 18. Benjamin Rush, Penn.; 19. Lyman Hall, Ga.; 20. John Rutledge, S.C.; 21. John Walton, Ga.; 22. George Washington, Va.; 23. John Penn, N.C.; 24. William Hooper, N.C.; 25. Richard Henry Lee, Va.; 26. George Wythe, Va.; 27. Thomas Jefferson, Va.

BIBLIOGRAPHY

Butterfield, L.H., editor. *Diary and Autobiography of John Adams.* Harvard University Press, Cambridge, Massachusetts: 1961.

Butterfield, L.H., M. Friedlander, and M. J. Kline, editors. *The Book of Abigail and John (Selected Letters).* Harvard University Press, Cambridge, Massachusetts: 1975.

Cappon, Lester J., editor. *The Adams-Jefferson Letters.* University of North Carolina Press, Chapel Hill: 1959.

Forbes, Esther. *Paul Revere & the World He Lived In.* Boston: Houghton Mifflin Co. 1942.

McCullough, David. *John Adams.* Simon and Schuster, New York: 2001.

Peabody, James Bishop, editor. *John Adams, A Biography in His Own Words.* Harper & Row, Publishers, Inc., New York: 1973.

ACKNOWLEDGMENTS

I wish to thank the good people at the reference desk of the North Independence branch of the Mid-Continent Public Library for their assistance, and my editor, Suzanne Patrick Fonda, for the fun of working with her. I completely recommend a visit to the Adams National Historical Park, 135 Adams Street, Quincy, Massachusetts 02169.

A NOTE ON THE QUOTATIONS

The quotations are taken from the letters and diaries of John and Abigail Adams as published in Butterfield, Friedlander, and Kline, and of Thomas Jefferson as published in Cappon, as well as from John's autobiography as edited by Butterfield. They were written at a time when our current notions of spelling and capitalization had not yet evolved.

Cheryl Harness does her illustrations on Strathmore cold-pressed illustration board, using watercolor, gouache, ink, and colored pencil.
Text is set in Celestia Antigua designed by Mark van Bronkhurst, MvB Design.
Library of Congress Cataloging-in-Publication Data
Harness, Cheryl.
The revolutionary John Adams / by Cheryl Harness.
p. cm.
Summary: A biography of John Adams with emphasis on his role in the American Revolution.
Includes bibliographical references.
ISBN 0-7922-6970-5
1. Adams, John, 1735-1826--Juvenile literature. 2. Presidents--United States--Biography--Juvenile literature. 3. Revolutionaries--United States--Biography--Juvenile literature. 4. United States--History--Revolution, 1775-1783--Biography--Juvenile literature. [1. Adams, John, 1735-1826. 2. Presidents. 3. United States--History--Revolution, 1775-1783.] I. Title.
E322 .H37 2003   973.3'092--dc21
2002011271

One of the world's largest nonprofit scientific and educational organizations, the National Geographic Society was founded in 1888 "for the increase and diffusion of geographic knowledge." Fulfilling this mission, the Society educates and inspires millions every day through its magazines, books, television programs, videos, maps and atlases, research grants, the National Geographic Bee, teacher workshops, and innovative classroom materials. The Society is supported through membership dues, charitable gifts, and income from the sale of its educational products. This support is vital to National Geographic's mission to increase global understanding and promote conservation of our planet through exploration, research, and education.

NATIONAL GEOGRAPHIC SOCIETY
1145 17th Street N.W. • Washington, D.C. 20036-4688 • U.S.A.
Visit the Society's Web site: www.nationalgeographic.com

Printed in Belgium